THE

GREAT AWAKENING'S

ASCENSION GUIDE

THE LIGHT HAS ALREADY WON

BY
DANIEL W. WINK

The Great Awakening's Ascension Guide

Published by D Wink Publishing

Uniontown, Arkansas

www.dwinkpublishing.com

ISBN:979-8-9997364-3-7

Printed in the United States of America

Library of Congress Cataloging-in-Publication Data

Daniel W Wink, 1954–

The Great Awakening's Ascension Guide /Daniel W Wink
p. cm.
ISBN 979-8-9997364-3-7

Spiritual life. 2. Consciousness. 3. Self-realization.
I. Title

I DEDICATE THIS BOOK TO MY LOVING SISTER, JOYCE MCINTOSH. JOYCE, YOU'VE BEEN ENCOURAGING ME TO WRITE THIS FOR A LONG TIME.

THE TIME HAS NEVER BEEN BETTER.

THANK YOU FOR YOUR SUPPORT SIS.

Preface

The time has come to end this long cycle of death and rebirth. We now hold in our hands the wisdom, and willingness, to rise above the shadows that have haunted humanity for ages.

In our desire to remain peaceful, we turned a blind eye to the evil among us. But it was that very **denial** that gave the evil the room to grow.

Evil cannot exist in the light. That is why it has always worked to keep us in the dark.

As long as we allow the inner darkness to go unhealed, the outer darkness will continue. So where do we go to find these shadows that have blinded us for so long? We go **within.**

Because the battlegrounds are not *"out there."* The battlegrounds are in our minds. And the mind is where we will win the battle.

We are reaching a turning point, one where many are beginning to realize: We have been prisoners of our own thoughts.

The world we see is a **projection** of that imprisoned thinking.

Not everyone will understand this, and that's okay. It only requires **enough** of us to make the difference.

We must stop waiting for permission to rise. *The Great Awakening* does not require all of humanity to be ready.

The time is now to go within, fully and deeply, and become the change we came here to bring.

This book was created to help you do that very thing. It offers you tools, practices, and reminders to support your inner journey.

Because when enough of us stop giving energy to a broken world, we can begin to **build a new one.**

Trying to fix this world with the same thinking that created it is like patching an old wine-skin with new skin. It tears.

Our old programming must be replaced, not repaired. What's needed now is not another solution from the past. What's needed,,,is a **new level of consciousness.**

And that begins with you.

That begins with us.

Love, Danny

Introduction

What happens when David Hawkins, EFT, and the New World Order collide?

You get, *The Great Awakening.*

Ever since the beginning of time, this world has been dominated by unseen forces, some ignorant, some intentionally evil.

This planet is a graveyard of civilizations that rose to power, only to crumble when their technology outpaced their spiritual growth. Humanity has advanced outwardly but forgotten to look inward.

We were never taught to turn within, to listen for the quiet presence of God that lives in each of us.

Instead, we were taught to seek answers, healing, and validation from outside sources.

We were conditioned to **depend on systems** that were never designed to set us free.

At this point in time, it no longer matters whether this deception was caused by evil intentions, or by well-meaning minds who simply didn't understand the harm they were doing. Because now, **we do understand.**

This cycle of evolution is different.

This time, something sacred is stirring. The veil of ignorance is lifting, and we are beginning to see:

Where we went wrong.
What we forgot.
And who we truly are.

We do not have to become another fallen civilization, buried in time for future generations to study and mourn what went wrong.

We can stop the cycle. We can choose again. We have the power to create a future where:

Negative emotions are remembered only as old myths.

Health is no longer compromised by poisons created for profit.
Scarcity and fear dissolve into abundance and peace.

We will live in a world where joy is normal, connections are sacred, and freedom is the air we breathe.

But there is a price, The price is not monetary, and it is not winning a war.

The price is,,,,,, inner work.

It will take the willingness of enough of us to turn within, face the shadows, and release the lies we have been carrying as truths. It will take courage to rise.
If enough of us are willing, the light will not just return, it will, **never leave again.**

This book brings together ancient wisdom, modern tools, and a fresh understanding of consciousness. What you're holding in your hand isn't just a guide, it's a mirror. One that reflects your own light back to you, until you remember, it was never lost.

Table of Contents

Chapter 1

The Great Awakening

Something big is happening all over the world. Some people are noticing it, others are not, but it's real. Weather the news talks about it or not.

People are calling it **"The Great Awakening."** For thousands of years, wise people have said this time would come. And now, it's finally here. Not some day out in the future, now. Right in front of us.

Most people don't really understand what's about to happen, and that's okay. Not everyone is ready for the changes that are about to occur. But those who are ready will feel it deep inside, their bodies, their dreams, and those quiet moments when they just know something is different.

As we grow and wake up on the inside, the world around us will start to change too.

We're not doing this alone, it's being guided by something far greater than us.

Fear is being replaced with love. Feeling like we don't have enough is turning into knowing there is more than enough. Sickness and pain won't be our futures anymore.

We're stepping into a new world, one where people live long, healthy, and happy lives. Not because of medicine or machines, but because we've remembered the truth about who we really are.

We might be the last generation to know what it feels like to experience a negative emotion. Things like anger, fear and guilt may well become things of the past.

The end of the heavens and the earth does not mean everything is going to be destroyed. It means there will be an end to a distinction between the two. It will be heaven on earth.

Now is the time to get ready and stay strong. Heaven is coming to earth. It's time to open our hearts and remember who we really are. What is about to happen is beyond anything we've seen. It's going to be big, and beautiful, and yes, it's going to be Biblical.

We can't ignore what's happening anymore. Right Now, the world is waking up. The people who have been secretly trying to control everything, the **Deep State,** the ones behind the scenes, are losing their power.

The truth is, the battle has already been won. The light has already taken control. It's just taking time to wake up the masses so they can see.

It's kind of like a chess game. Even before the last piece is moved, both sides can see how it's going to end. The ones trying to hold on to power know they've lost. But like the sore losers they are, they are trying to cause as much trouble as they can on their way out.

But things are changing fast.

#######

People all around the world are waking up. Together, our minds and hearts are rising. And the energy, that rising awareness, is like a giant ocean. Deep, alive, and full of light.

Each of us is like a drop of water in that great ocean.

This book is here to help you choose where in this ocean you what your drop of water to be. Will you rise to the top? Where the water is nice and clear, warm, and full of life?

Or will your drop stay near the bottom, where it's dark and heavy? Full of sediment from things that should have been long forgotten.

The answer is simple:

Let us rise to the clearer water.

Chapter 2

The New World Order

There isn't a company or building named, **"The New World Order."** It's not something we can shut down or vote out of office like a normal group or government organization. Instead, it's an idea, a way of thinking.

It's a pattern of thought that keeps showing up, where certain people or groups try to control the masses.

These people show up in systems that want everyone they think is less than them, to feel afraid, guilty and ashamed.

Their goal is to pull the strings behind the scenes, to gain power, and crush any uniqueness,. They want to keep us distracted so we forget how to look within and remember who we really are inside.

Groups like the **Bilderberg Group,** the **World Economic Forum** and even the **United Nations** are examples of the kind of people that are pushing a darker plan onto the world.

#######

In the big ocean of human thought and feelings, what we call the collective consciousness, their plan is to keep stirring up the mud from the bottom of this ocean. They don't want us to rise up and see the light.

They want us stuck in the lower levels of energy, where fear is in charge and real freedom feels too far away. This is where we are the easiest to trick and control.

They whisper lies into our ears, hoping we will believe them. "Let us decide what is best for you." "Your not smart enough to know what is best." You're not good enough." You need us to protect you." "Just follow the rules, and you'll be safe." Be Safe? Safe from what? The truth is, the only thing we need protection from is them.

#######

A long time ago, when people had big questions, they didn't go online. They went within. They prayed. They listened. They trusted that still small voice within to receive wise guidance.

But now, the people in power want us to turn to technology to get our answers. Their technology. Technology they program.

Through it, they can control what we see, what we hear, and even what we are lead to believe.

Even our schools are controlled by these nefarious people. With huge amounts of money, especially from the **Rockefeller family,** a new kind of education system was created.It wasn't built to help the kids discover their gifts or talents. It was built to train the children in how to follow orders. They had one goal, prepare the people for factory work.

One group, the ***General Education Board,*** helped reshape schools to fit the needs of factories, not the dreams of our souls.

One advisor even said something chilling.

"We won't try to make these kids into deep thinkers or scientists. Our job is simple. We will train them to do perfectly what their parents did imperfectly."

It was never just about owning land or making laws. It was always about controlling how people think. Control what kids learn, and you control their minds. Control the food, and you control their health. Control the media, and you control the stories they believe.

And by controlling the chemicals in our food and air, they are blocking something even deeper, the part of us that's connected to God. That sacred spark that can't be owned, bought, or broken. Yes, they are that evil.

Chapter 3

The Battle for Our Souls

The battle has already begun. Each side has made it's choice. Now it's your turn: Which side are you on?

Will you take the sacred journey within, living with an open heart, guided by the quiet voice inside you? Or will you follow the path of fear, controlled by lies, fake leaders, and machines that try to think for you?

Everything in the universe is made of vibrations. Vibration is like the invisible framework that shapes what we see and feel. It is the hum beneath everything.

The people who want to control the world, what we call the **Deep State** or the **Illuminati,** feed off the lower vibrations, of fear, shame and guilt. That's the dark energy they use to create the world they can control. This is why they need the people to stay stuck in their negative emotions.

But here's the secret:

If we stop living in those lower vibrations, we stop feeding them the energy they need to survive.

No fear = no fuel for darkness.

When we rise into love, truth, and joy, their false world falls apart.

One of the most important tools for understanding this is a book by Dr. David Hawkins called, ***"Power vs. Force."***

In a world full of confusion, this book is like a flashlight in the dark.

Dr. Hawkins showed us that truth is a measurable energy frequency. And the energy can be tested using a method called muscle testing or kinesiology.

He created something known as the **"Map of Consciousness",** a scale that goes from 0 to 1,000 that shows the level of integrity of anything we live with.

And what did he discover? Truth has power. Integrity has power. Your body can feel the difference between truth and falsehood.

Your heart already knows the difference between truth and falsehood. You don't need permission from anyone. You don't need a priest, a guru, or a phone line to heaven. You already have the code. It's inside you. You don't need to *"call the man"*.

You are *the man*.

All you have to do, is listen to the voice within.

Chapter 4

Muscle Testing

Do you want to excess to your inner truth detector? Here's how:

I'm sharing this in the beginning of this book so you don't have to take my word, or anybody else's opinion for what is true. You deserve the right to test it for yourself.

Even the Bible tells us to watch out for false teachers. And let's be honest, we've all been getting fooled long enough.

Dr. David Hawkins, ***"Map of Consciousness"***, shows different levels of energy based on the different kinds of human thoughts and emotions. If your level of consciousness is above 200 on the map of consciousness, you have the ability to sense what is true and what is false. But here's the deal:

You must be honestly searching for the truth. Not just trying to prove you are right. If you are only looking to validate your opinion, your energy drops, and your results won't be accurate.

Ready to try it? Here are three simple ways to test truth with your body.

Arm test (Classic Muscle Testing)

Hold one arm straight out from your side. Say an affirmative statement, out loud or in your mind. Have someone gently push down on your arm using two fingers. If your arm stays strong, the statement is true. If your arm drops or feels weak, the statement is false.

Finger Loop Test

Touch your thumb and ring finger together to make a loop. Put your index finger from your other hand inside the loop. Say your statement. Try to pull your index finger through the loop.

If the loop holds strong, the statement is true. If your fingers break apart, the statement is false.

Sway Test (Body Compass)

Stand relaxed with your heals close together. Make a statement like,

I am a man/woman.

If the statement is true, you will feel you body lean forward. If the statement is false, you will lean backwards.

Tip: When you make your statement, start it with, **"For the highest Good."** Than make your statement.

This will help you set a clean, honest intention, not from ego or fear, but from your higher self.

#######

If these techniques aren't working for you, your energy may be scrambled. If that's the case you just need a reset.

The Thymus Thump

Smile and thump the center of your chest (over your heart) three times.

Each time you tap say out loud: "Ha Ha Ha, Ha Ha Ha, Ha Ha Ha Three times.

This helps reset your energy and unscrambles it. Try it now and see if you feel a shift.

Ways to use this

Let's say you're in a bookstore looking for a book on healing. You find you have ten books to chose from. How do you know which one is best for you?

Try This:

Hold a book or hold it in your thoughts and ask,

"For the highest good, is this the right book for me?"

Then pause.

Does you body lean forward or backwards? Try the finger loop method. Do your fingers hold strong or slip right through?

Every book will carry the energy level of where it calibrates on the *"Map of Consciousness"*. Some will be based on the author's ego, others will come from deeper truths. The higher the energy, the more helpful it will be for your journey.

Let your body be your compass. The more you listen to it, the clearer your answers will become.

This can be used to help you pick your fruit in the produce department.

Jesus said to pray constantly. Prayer isn't just speaking. It's about turning within to listen to your heart and following your divine guidance. Constant prayer is listening to your inner signals. And Truth? Truth is always whispering.

Your job is simple;

Listen

Chapter 5

The Map of Consciousness

Dr. David Hawkins' ***"Map of Consciousness"*** is a gift to humanity.

David created something amazing. A map that shows the full range of human emotions and spiritual states of consciousness. It runs from the lowest, most painful states to the highest, most divine levels of awareness.

This scale runs from 0 to 1,000. Each state of mind has a vibrational frequency, a kind of invisible energy. Each level connects to a certain emotion, a way of thinking, and a way of living.

Key levels on the Map

20 - Shame: The lowest energy. Feeling worthless.

30 - Guilt: Regret, blame, and punishing yourself.

50 - Apathy: Hopelessness. "Nothing I do matters"

75 - Grief: Sadness and loss.

100 - Fear: Anxiety and always trying to stay in control

125 - Desire: Obsession with things. Craving more.

150 - Anger: Frustration, resentment.

175 - Pride: Thinking you're better than others.

The Turning Point

200- Courage: This is the game-changer. You stop running From life and start facing it. You begin to Grow real strength. This is the level where people stop being controlled by fear.

Below 200, life is about your past.
Above 200, life becomes about your future.

Higher States of Being

250 - Neutrality: Calm and flexible. Not easily thrown off.

310 - Willingness: Ready to learn and grow.

350 - Acceptance: Letting go of blame.

400 - Reason: Clear thinking, logic, and intelligence.

500 - Love: Unconditional love, kindness, and seeing all as One.
Where *"The Experiential Life"* begins.
Some call this *"5D Consciousness"*

540 - Bliss: Pure joy, beauty, and grace.

600 - Peace: Deep stillness. Oneness with all.

650 - Healing: Transformation at the soul level.

700 - 1,000 Enlightenment: Complete unity with God. This is the level of saints, sages, and Enlightened beings. Such as: Jesus, Buddha, And Krishna. They didn't just teach the truth. They were the truth. To reach this level the Ego has to disappear. Only love remains.

A living Metaphor

Hold your hand out with your fingers extended, and relaxed. Think of this as being at peace. That calibrates at 600 on the *"Map of Consciousness"*. Now clench your hand into a fist. Think of this as being shame. That calibrates at 20.

Being stuck in either position, with your hand wide open or in a fist is just as crippling. You don't want to be stuck in either position..

The goal isn't to always be peaceful. You want to be able to move freely between states of consciousness as needed.

I can go into a very blissful state. You don't me driving then.

Even Jesus, known as the Prince of Peace, got angry a lot. Like when he flipped tables over in the temple. One time he even cussed out a fig tree and killed it.

Sometimes anger is needed. It can motivate action, but you don't want to be stuck there.

You want to experience whatever sensation that is currently passing through your body. Experience it and then let it go. You don't want to identify with it. You are not angry. You are a divine being that is temporarily experiencing anger.

There is a big difference between experiencing an emotion and identifying as the emotion. You are not your emotions.

A Note on Being Human

Even if you live above 200 on the *"Map of Consciousness"*, you will still feel anger, fear, or grief at times. It does not mean you have failed. It means you are human.

Every time you show courage, you are making a breakthrough. Every time you forgive someone, you are lifting the world. Every time you choose love, you are tipping the balance for everyone.

It all matters. Let your body be your compass. Let your conscious be your guide.

Chapter 6

Journey from 200 to 500

200 should represent adulthood

This is where you take responsibility for yourself. You become inner directed, and you are ready to perceive your own dreams.

In the 250 area of the *"Map of Consciousness"* stop allowing your negative emotions to control you anymore. You see you have a future that is independent of the people you used to rely on as a child.

Today this line into adulthood is very blurry, but at least now it is being recognized. We have a lot of people that are in their thirties and forties that have never reached maturity. They still act and think like they need to be taken care of.

#######

Years ago and in other cultures, there used to be rituals for when a child reached a certain age it was acknowledged by his tribe that he was now an adult. Today we have no such rituals to welcome the child into adulthood. When does a boy know in his mind that he's a man? He needs to know. A boy should be told by his father, that he is now a man.

Today we have fathers that never got the acknowledgment from their fathers. This is a cultural problem that can be fixed with understanding. Like every truth, it will be healed when the misunderstanding is brought into the light.

#######

Above 200 on the ***"Map of Consciousness"*** you begin filtering your beliefs instead of letting them filter you. You start asking questions like:

"Is this belief helping me grow?" "Does this still feel right for who I'm becoming?" Little by little you start letting go of the ones that no longer serve you.

In the past, this was hard to do. Most people avoided the process because there wasn't a clear way to do it. This is the reason spiritual growth felt so out of reach for many.

Another trap that was created by the ***"Deep State"*** was established religions. Yes, this battle goes back that far. The individual has always had this calling within to connect with their source. The people that wanted control over the masses used this desire to manipulate and establish control. Religion say, ***"Let me tell you what to think."*** A true spiritual teacher should be saying, ***"Let me show you how to think."*** There's a big difference.

#######

That's Why This Book Exist. To help you make your journey a lot smoother. To help you grow by letting go of beliefs that no longer serve you. Freedom doesn't come from holding on to things that were never yours to begin with. It comes from releasing attachments, especially the ones tied to old beliefs that are holding you back.

Some beliefs are easy to let of. Others feel personal, like giving them up would mean losing a part of yourself but letting go is how you rise.

Retiring beliefs that no longer serve you is a major obstacle you must overcome if you want to grow to any degree at all.

A question that will come up is, how many of these beliefs are mine, and how many of them are someone else's, that I have been holding on to so I can fit in.

You must deal with people that have an investment in you maintaining some beliefs. This can be disguised as family or religious loyalty.

Jesus warned of these kinds of divisions be created. He said, "Think not that I come to send peace on earth: I came not to send peace, but a sword. For I come to set man at odds with his father, and daughter against her mother."

It may sound harsh, but he wasn't trying to start division. He was predicting what will happen when truth enters a world of illusions.

One of the most dangerous forces in the world is blind obedience. He was saying we can not just go along to get along.

When someone in the family wakes up and starts living from love instead of fear. It can make others uncomfortable. Why? Because now they have see this person differently.

When you grow, others will have to change too, and they don't want to be moved out of their comfort zones. So, they blame you. But their discomfort is not your burden to carry. You're not here to keep others comfortable. You're here to wake up, to rise, to love, and to live in truth. And Truth? Truth sets everyone free, even if it stings at first.

The power of Courage

200 on the *"Map of Consciousness"* is where people stop being blindly obedient and start thinking for themselves. They stop numbing themselves with drugs and alcohol and start asking the bigger questions.

This is where people take control of their power. At 200 is where the *"Deep State"* loose their control over you. The *"Deep State"* can only control people who are stuck in fear, guilt and shame. Once someone rises above 200, they wake up and wont believe the lies anymore.

Chapter 7

The Experiential State

When Jesus was ask, where is the Kingdom of God, he didn't say, **"You'll go there after you die."** He Said,

"The Kingdom of God is within you"

He was talking about living in the now. Not some future, far away time. Heaven and hell are not places we will go after we die. They are states of consciousness that we choose to live in now.

You are choosing your *"Location"* every moment, based on your currently dominate thoughts.

Heaven, Hell, and Purgatory on the Map

Living below 200 on the **"Map on Consciousness"** is the equivalent to living in Hell. Guilt, shame, and all the negative emotions that make life a living hell.

Living above 500 on the **"Map of Consciousness"** is the equivalent to living in Heaven. Peace, Love and joy, and experiencing oneness with God.

Living in the area between 200 and 500 on the **"Map of Consciousness"** is the equivalent to living in Purgatory. It's the place where we cleanse and purify ourselves.

Heaven or Hell = Love or Fear

According to Dr. Hawkins, there are over 400 billion vibrational frequencies that a person can experience while in a physical body. However the body can only experience a span of 2,000 frequencies at a time. This is why you can not experience love and fear that the same time. The frequencies are too far apart.

Have you ever loved someone so much you couldn't see anything wrong with them? Everything is wonderful. Later you look at them and think, What did I ever see in this person? They didn't change, you did. You were coming from a different frequency.

Parallel Universes

Imagine you're at a crowed fair. You can see families laughing, eating snacks, and enjoying each others company. In that same area you may see drug dealers selling drugs to addicts, and hookers finding johns.

Those living in joy see other joyful people. They don't even notice the other things going on. Different levels of consciousness existing in the same space, at the same time, side be side. They don't notice each other because they're vibrating on different frequencies.

A Global Shift is Already Taking Place

Dr. Hawkins wrote, In 1986 for the first time in history, the collective consciousness of mankind has risen above 200.

That moment is when the future of mankind changed forever. No longer are we content being blindly obedient to governments, religions, or any other curtains the **"Deep State"** wants to hind behind.

This was the moment when Toto pulled back the curtain.

The Great Shift

Now that the curtain has been pulled back there has been a constant drip, drip, drip of information that has been coming out. We are constantly being exposed to more and more truth all the time.

Do to all the fear that we have ingrained with, God is being very kind, not exposing everything at one time.

However this drip is about to turn into a flood. The results of this flood will be a physical splitting of the earth. There will be two worlds.

This book is an attempt to help you prepare for the "**New World**".

Jesus and The Frequency of Love

When Jesus walked the earth, the collective consciousness was around 100. Today the collective consciousness is around 205. This is a huge shift.

When Jesus was talking to the people about going to heaven, he had to use parables to try to get the message across.

We had a man that calibrated at 1,000, talking to people that calibrated at 100. His message was to tell them what their lives would be like if they would learn to live at 500.

That was a big job. To this day it's hard to explain what it's like above 500.

The Experiential Life

Above 500 you stop, *"thinking about life"*. You start experiencing it. You feel connected to everything. Words loose their ability to explain what you are feeling.

The sensation is like an energy flowing freely through you, and any attempt you try to control this flow obstructs it, and cuts it off. It's through total surrender to this energy where heaven is found.

Letting Go of the Ego

From 200 to 500 on the *"Map of Consciousness"* the mind is in charge. It wants proof, facts, and explanations.

Above 500, things can not be proven. Can you prove to me you love someone? Of course not. It is beyond words. There is a whole world above words. It's just your rational mind don't want you to see it. Why? Because it's not it's world.

At these levels, you no longer identify with the body. You're still in the body, but you don't think it is what you are.

You become a vessel for something greater. As you get closer to 500, you begin to see through the illusions of the world.

Swapping beliefs become like rearranging the deck chairs on the Titanic, it won't save the ship. Eventually, even the best version of yourself, your polished ego, must go.

Beliefs are boats

Religions and other belief systems are like canoes. Think of your destination being on the other side of the stream. They help you cross the stream. They have value in helping you on your journey.

Once you can reach the other shore, you have to let go of the canoe. Now that your on dry land, the canoe serves no purpose. Living in the now means letting go of the past, including old ideas, roles, and identities,

"Please forget me, so that we may meet in Heaven"

You make a Difference

If you are sitting at home wondering if your spiritual growth really matters in the big picture. The answer is YES.

You are a part of the collective consciousness. Any growth you achieve sends ripples through the whole world. Your frequency helps lift the entire planet.

How one Person's Energy Affects The Collective Consciousness

Some of the findings made by Dr. Hawkins.

One Person who calibrates at 300 counterbalances the negativity of 90,000 people stuck below 200.

One Person who calibrates at 400 counterbalances the negativity of 400,000 people stuck below 200.

One Person who calibrates at 500 counterbalances the negativity of 750,000 people stuck below 200.

One Person who calibrates at 600 counterbalances the negativity of 10 million people stuck below 200.

One Person who calibrates at 700 counterbalances the negativity of 12 million people stuck below 200.

One Person who calibrates at 1,000 counterbalances the negativity of 70 million people stuck below 200.

Your light matters more than you can imagine,
Keep rising, Keep loving.
The world is shifting and you are helping by leading the way

Chapter 8

The Hundredth Monkey

Back in the 1950s scientist noticed something strange on a small island called Koshima.

A young monkey started doing something new. She began washing her sweet potatoes in the ocean to clean off the dirt before eating them.

Other monkeys saw her doing this and started to do the same thing.

Eventually most of the monkeys on this one island were washing there potatoes before eating them.

Then something amazing happened.

Once enough monkeys on this one island learned this new habit, legend says it was about the hundredth monkey, suddenly, monkeys on other islands started doing the same thing.

Islands hundreds of miles away.

These monkeys hadn't seen this behavior before. No one had taught them. So how did they learn this?

The Answer: The Collective Consciousness. The shift didn't spread through talking or logic. It spread through something deeper, a shared awareness that connected them all.

This is called **"The Critical Mass"**. The point where when enough minds or hearts shift in a collective cause, the entire field changes.

You Might be the Hundredth Monkey.

That is why your awakening matters. Because when enough people wake up, the world will change. The rules will shift. The future opens to the **"New World"**. You might be the one that tips the scale.

You could be the hundredth monkey.

Chapter 9

The Aquarium

Picture a giant glass aquarium, so tall you can't see the top, and so wide it goes on forever.

It's filled with water. This water represents the collective consciousness. The shared energy and awareness of everyone on earth.

Etched in the glass side of the aquarium are horizontal lines that reach all the way up the side. Each line represents a different vibrational frequency as it goes up the scale. One line for each frequency that can be experienced while in the human body.

There are vibrational frequencies that go beyond the top of this tank, but the human body isn't built to handle those energy levels. They are too strong.

So while we're here in these bodies, we're limited to move through the levels that are within the tank.

The Higher You Go, The Lighter It Gets

At the top of the tank, the water is clear and bright. Pure and full of light. But as you go lower, the water becomes darker, heavier, and cloudy.

What Makes The Water Cloudy?

That's sediment caused by old pains, fears, guilt and shame.

These are beliefs that are not true. It's like spiritual dirt. It sticks to you and pulls you down. **You Are a Drop of Water** in this tank.

Your soul is a drop of water floating inside this huge tank. Where your drop floats depends on how much, and what kind, of sediment you are clinging onto.

If you have a lot of sediment, you will sink lower. If you have less sediment, you will float higher. People floating around you will have the same amount of sediment as you do. Look down and you'll see others weighed down with more. Look up, and you'll see drops floating more freely towards the light.

The Tipping Point: Level 200

If your drop of water rises above 200 on the **"Map on Consciousness"**, you start to see the light filtering down from above. You feel it in your soul, like a quiet pull upwards. That's your call to rise.

But if your stuck below 200, the water is so murky it's hard to even imagine the light above existing. You can't see the way out. You only see the sediment around you.

That's why I Wrote This Book

This book is like a flashlight shining a way to the higher waters.

A lifeline. A whisper saying, "This way".

You don't have to fight or struggle. You only have to let go of the things that are weighing you down. That sediment.

This sediment is made of your own thoughts and beliefs. The ones that whisper to you at night. The ones that say, "This is just how life is."

But here's the Truth:

By letting go of your negative beliefs, you will naturally float higher.

Let go of anger, and the water gets clearer.

Forgive someone, and you rise a little bit more.

The more you release, the closer you get to the light.

The light is there, waiting for you.

Chapter 10

The Healing Power of EFT

Over the years, I've studied many different healing techniques. My favorite one by far is EFT.
Emotional Freedom Techniques

This is a simple technique and anyone can do it. You don't need any special training or years of practice. In just one evening, you can learn it and get results.

Other healing methods I learned was about mastering my energy then projecting it to others. EFT is different. It showed me how to teach others how to control their own energy. With this process, no one needs to rely on me or anyone else. They don't even need to believe in the technique to get results. They only need to do it.

This is not "Faith Healing"

If you do the process, it works, even if your skeptical. Honestly, I love working with people who don't believe it will work. That moment after the tapping session, when they feel the results.

They get that look on their face, like, wait, what just happened? It's Priceless.

That's when they're ready to listen.

A True Story

One day I was having a tapping session with a lady and her husband was sitting across the room and he was a real doubting Thomas. Arms crossed and not interested at all. His energy was kind of a distracting. So I ask him, "Do you have any problems I could help you with?" He said, ***"Nope."***

His wife quickly added, *"He has terrible back pain."* I ask if he'd be willing to give it a try? He shrugged and said, *"I guess so."* After a couple rounds of tapping, his back pain was gone. I ask him if he had any other issues.

He said that has hands were numb. They have been for years. Ever since he had surgery for carpal tunnel. So we tapped on the lack of feeling in his hands, and the feelings came back. He kept opening and closing his fist saying, *"That's amazing."*

A few months later we were talking on the phone and he told me he had to start using potholders again, now that he had feeling back in his hands, he could feel the heat again.

How EFT Works

EFT helps you release emotional baggage. It clears the "sediment" that keeps your drop of water stuck in the lower levels of the aquarium.

About 80 to 90% of all physical illnesses start with emotional pain.

Your body isn't betraying you. It's sending you messages:

"Something inside needs your attention"

We are the creators of our bodies. The bodies give us a place to feel, to learn, and to experience the results of our thoughts.

You are not just a body. Your consciousness, is a field of awareness.

The body is a hologram that your thoughts created. You think, and your body responds. Your body is a reflection of your thoughts.

You are spirit. The Bible says that we we're created in the image of God. God is a creative spirit. You are a creative spirit.

Negative emotions cause blockages in your spiritual bodies lymphatic system. When your system gets a block, EFT helps remove it,

A block is just something inside that needs your attention.

If you gently tap on specific energy points, called meridian points, the blocks dissolves. Just like that.

You don't need to rely on anyone else for your health. You can use this technique anytime, and you can even use it to help others.

Experience It for Yourself.

There is a saying:

"I Hear, I Forget. I See, I Remember. I do, I understand"

And not a moment before.

If you only read this book, your mind might remember what I said. But, your body won't understand the experience. You'll stay stuck in your head, and your ego loves that idea. The ego loves to think, judging, and staying stuck in indecision. But when you actually do the work, when you enter what's called the, *"The Experiential States of Consciousness"*.

You stop wanting to overthink things.

You start to know.

And that's when the ego fades into the background, where it belongs.

Chapter 11

Tapping Points

When you tap these points on your body, you send tiny vibrations through your meridian system, an energy pathway that runs through your body. These vibrations help to release stuck energy, emotions, and stress.

Let's go over the tapping points, one by one.

The Karate Chop Point

This is the starting point for every tapping session. It's located on the side of your hand, right below your pinky finger, the spot you'd use to do a karate chop.

What you say while tapping this point is very important, It sets the tone for the whole process.

We'll come back to what to say in just a bit.

The Top of the Head

Gently tap the top of your head. Tap just hard enough where you can hear it.

Do this about 6 or 7 times.

The Beginning of the Eyebrow

Tap where your eyebrow starts, near the bridge of your nose.

Daniel W. Wink

The Side of the Eye

Tap the bone at the side of the eye, right next to the outer corner, where the eye socket begins

Under the Eye

Tap the spot right under your eye, where those little puffy bags show up when you don't get enough sleep.

Under the Nose

Tap the area between your nose and your upper lip.

The Chin Point

Tap the dip between your bottom lip and your chin.

The Collarbone Area

Tap about an inch below where your collarbone begins in the center of your chest

Under the Arm

Tap under the arm, about where a bra strap would be, around 3 or 4 inches below the armpit.

Wrist Point

Finally, tap the inside of your wrist, on the same side as your palm.

Some Tips

Remove glasses if they have a wire across the bridge of the nose. They can block the energy flow. And remove any quartz watches during the tapping session.They might interfere with your body's natural

Chapter 12

Tapping Session

Let's try a Quick Tapping Session. This will only take a minute, and it's simple.

Let's say you have a back pain. That's what we will focus on for this example.

Step 1: Check How You Feel

While standing bend over to touch your toes. Don't push yourself, just see how far you can go. Does it hurt? On a scale of 1 to 10, How bad is the pain? How far did you reach? This gives you a baseline of where you're starting.

Now take a seat.
Remove your watch and glasses if you're wearing them.

Step 2: Karate Chop Point

Start tapping the side of your hand, just below your pinky. This is the karate chop point. As you tap say:

"Even though my back really hurts, I deeply and completely love and accept myself"

"Even though my back really hurts, I deeply and completely love and accept myself"

"Even though my back really hurts, I deeply and completely love and accept myself"

Your back might not hurt that bad right now, that's okay. Let's see what happens. Memories of old pains you had in the past might come up. Let them. That's what you're looking for. This is part of the healing process.

Try saying, **"Even though my back pain is really killing me,"** and see if this stirs anything up. The more emotions or sensations you can dig up, the better. Go ahead and say it. The more emotions you can feel, the more thorough the healing will be.

Step 3: Go Through the Tapping Points

Now tap each of the following points while saying:

"Really Painful."
Tap about 6-7 times at each spot:
Top of the Head: **"Really Painful"**
Beginning of the Eyebrow: **"Really Painful"**
Side of the Eye: **"Really Painful"**
Under the Eye: **"Really Painful"**
Under the Nose: **"Really Painful"**
On the Chin: **"Really Painful"**
On the Collarbone: **"Really Painful"**
Under the Arm: **"Really Painful"**
Inside the wrist: **"Really Painful"**

Step 4: Relax & Recheck

Now take a deep breath and exhale.
Let it all sink in.
Stand up again and try touching your toes.
How far did you reach this time?
What's your pain level now, on the scale of 1 to 10?
Are you feeling better?
And that was just one round, which only takes about a minute.
EFT works on everything.
Back pain is an example.
You can use EFT for any kind of pain, be it physical or emotional.

You can even use EFT for someone else through something called surrogate tapping.

Surrogate Tapping

Think of someone who's in need of a treatment. Go through the tapping process as if you were that person. It's surprising how well this works with a little practice.

One Important Note

For EFT to work, the person who is receiving the treatment weather it's you or someone else, needs to be willing to let go of the issue that is being addressed. Sometimes people hold on to their issues because they are getting something out of being unwell. This is called secondary gain.

For Example:

A person with a back pain could be getting out of a lot of work due to their pain. They may not want to be healed. Someone who is sick might be getting some extra attention and love from family and friends, so part of them may not want this to stop.

Chapter 13

Tap Tap Tap

A full round of tapping only takes about one minute, which means in an hour, you can work through a lot of things.

There are a lot of things stored up in your subconscious mind. Old emotions, buried memories, limiting beliefs, all that's just waiting to be released.

We'll talk more about some of those things later. But for now, just keep tapping.

#######

Have you ever used an old well hand-pump? At first you have to pump like crazy just to get the water to start flowing.

But once the water starts flowing, you can slow down and the water will flow in a nice steady stream.

Tapping is the same way. At first it might feel like your energy is sluggish running through your system. Then suddenly, whoosh, the energy starts moving.

Your body is ready to talk. If you've never done energy work before, tapping is like opening a brand-new way to have a conversation with your body.

You're asking: ***"Can we talk?"***
And your body say: ***"I'm so glad you ask."***

As you tap, all kinds of things will come up, old memories, feelings, even aches and pains you thought were ***"Just a part of life."*** That's a good sign. You're stirring up the sediment in your drop of water.

Your body is saying: ***"Here's what I've been holding on to."*** And you say: ***"I hear you, let's take care of these things."***

And that, right here, is the beginning of healing. Building a connection with your body as you keep tapping, you will start to recognize your inner signals talking to you. Your body will tell you when something is off.

You'll feel when your inner child is asking for attention. The more you listen, the stronger your connection will become. Eventually, your body will trust that you're listening now.

And here's the cool part: The stronger the connection gets, the less you will need to tap. Soon you will be able to release an emotion or issue just by noticing it., With thought alone. That's how powerful this work is. It's like the old well: Once the water starts flowing, you don't need to pump so hard.

Real-Life Examples

I don't tap that often anymore, but it's still good to have it in my muscle memory. Sometimes while I'm working in the yard I get attacked by a bunch of wasps.

Stings everywhere, this really hurts. Right away, I start tapping. From head to wrist, I tap until the pain eases. In just a few minutes the pain is gone. It's like I was never stung.

Another time, I twisted my ankle. I sat down and tapped. The pain went down quickly, and I was back on my feet and working in no time. No limping around on crutches for a few days this time.

You may not need to tap every point every time. As you practice, you may find that just tapping a few points is enough to get the relief you want. The key is to listen to your body and trust the process. You're learning a new way to connect, heal, and grow, and your body is right there with you.

Chapter 14

The Power of Even Though

Every tapping session should start at the karate point.
While tapping this spot, say a setup phrase that begins with:

"Even though I" or *"Even though my"*

This is where you name the issue you want to work on.
It's like stepping up and telling your body;

"Here is what we are going to release"

This is where you get honest with yourself. No pretending,
no hiding, just lay your cards on the table. Let's return to the
back pain example. Start by saying something like:

"Even though I have this back pain, I deeply and completely love and accept myself."

Then pause and listen to your thoughts. Does anything come
up? Is the pain the result of an accident?

"Even though I was in this terrible accident"

Did the back pain start after being passed over for a
promotion?

"Even though I feel like I'm being held back"

"Even though I see no way to move forward"

"Even though I feel like I'm trapped"

"Even though my future seems bleak to me"

Let your mind dig. See what memories or emotions come up. Many times the pain starts after something happened. Maybe right away, or maybe months or a year later.

Your not looking for anything you have to validate why you feel it. This is a conversation between you and your body. If you feel someone caused you the pain, you do not have to justify or validate your feelings to them or anyone else in anyway.

Your not trying to figure out why it happened, you're looking for emotional energy that has been blocked or suppressed.

The more you feel the emotional charge, the better it will clear. Try to intensify the feelings while you tap the karate chop. Let the emotions rise. Any frustration, sadness, fear, anger,whatever is there. The stronger the emotional reaction, the better the release will be. That's how you clear it from your energy system.

Why "Even Though" Works So Well

Saying "Even though" helps you avoid something called psychological reversal. That's when your subconscious mind tries to fight what you are trying to do.

Lets' say you're trying to lose 10 pounds. So, you say,

"I am going to lose 10 pounds."

But your subconscious mind says, **"Yeah, right. You tried that before and you gained 10 pounds."**

Your mind rejects the affirmation, and now you're stuck.

But if you said:

"Even though I Want to lose 10 pounds, I deeply and completely love and accept myself."

There's nothing for the subconscious mind to object to. You're acknowledging the truth and offering compassion at the same time.

Why the Ending is so Powerful

Ending your statement with:

"I deeply and completely love and accept myself,"

This is giving your subconscious mind another option.

You're not just removing a negative response, your giving your subconscious mind a healthier and more loving response to turn to in the future.
   When given a choice, your subconscious mind will always pick the belief that is most beneficial to you.

Chapter 15

Just Learn How to Talk

I'm just a good old southern boy with an 8ᵗʰ grade education. Then I went and married a woman from Wisconsin with a master's degree in journalism.

You can probably guess where this is going. I'd say something, and she'd correct my English. Every time, boom, instant anger.

It would come out of nowhere. I wasn't thinking clearly. I was being triggered by old, buried emotions.

When I was in Toastmasters, The other members would mention how I talked. I told them I always had a problem with spelling, then I realized. Spelling would be a whole lot easier if I'd just learn how to talk right.

At first, I figured it was just my southern accent. I couldn't give up my southern charm, could I?

The First Big Test

One day while I was learning EFT, I said something and my wife corrected my speech. Just like clock work my buttons were pushed.

I knew this was my chance to test this EFT out on something real. Let's see if it works as well as Gary Craig says it does. Gary Craig was the creator of EFT.

So I went out to the garage and found myself a chair and took a seat.

I tapped on my karate chop point and said:

"Even Though she makes me angry, I deeply and completely love and accept myself."

"Even Though she makes me angry, I deeply and completely love and accept myself."

"Even Though she makes me angry, I deeply and completely love and accept myself."

I tapped through the cycle and sure enough the anger was gone. That was a good start but I still had a ways to go with this. For one thing, I started with **Blame.**

On the *"Map of Consciousness"* Blame calibrates at 30. Not a good place to be.

I knew if I truly wanted to heal this behavior I had to take responsibility for my own emotions, which means no blame is allowed.

This move right there took the situation from 30 to 200.

Now I was in a position where I can act responsibly.

If I stayed in blame I would have to find a way to change her to find relief. Taking responsibility put me in a position where it didn't concern her at all.

So I continued down the rabbit whole.

"She made me angry"

"What did she do that made me angry?"

That was simple. She criticized me.

"So I don't like being criticized?"

"Why did I react so strongly to criticism?

#######

See your mate as your mirror

Close relationships brings up stuff. Guy's, you tell your wife something and she will get to work poking holes in it.

It's not that she wants you to fail. It's not that she doesn't want to support you.

Think of it as she is helping you test your vision for weak spots. She might not even be doing this on a conscious level.

What she is doing is testing your vision and if you can't get through her, it's not going far. She's a proof tester.

I once told my wife that I would like to do some public speaking. I guess she saw that as a sign to help me get ready.

So, I tapped

#######

"Even though I don't like being criticized, I deeply and completely love and accept myself."

I repeated that 3 times. As I said this I felt tightness in my eyes and forehead. This was a sign to me that energy blockages were being discovered. So than I ask,

"Where did I learn to hate criticism so bad?"

I had to learn it somewhere. It came to me that when I was a small boy, my big brother used to criticize me all the time, and it was usually followed with a beating.

So every time someone criticized me, my subconscious mind got ready for the oncoming beating.

"Get ready, Your about to get punished"

That's what my body was reacting to. So I tapped a few rounds about that. After that I was ready for the next question.

"What is criticism Anyways?"

It's just allowing someone else s opinion to be more important than my own.
So, I tapped

"Even though I let someone else s opinion be more important than my own, I deeply and completely love and accept myself."

I repeated that 3 times.

Since then, criticism rarely bothers me anymore. It still shows up on very rare occasions but very rarely

Most of the time, I just sing,

"You say tomato, I say tamaato."

No more anger.
No more hurt.
Just peace..

Chapter 16

Karma

A lot of people misunderstand what karma is. They think it's about getting punished for something they did that was bad in the past. Like the universe is waiting to get revenge.

But that's not what karma is about. Karma isn't about punishment. It's about balance. It's about healing. It's about letting go. It's about finally being free from the things you've been holding onto for far too long.

Karma is about Resolution. Karma doesn't come back to hurt you, it comes back to wake you up.

It's like your soul is saying,

"Hey, there's something here that hasn't been dealt with yet. Let's take care of it so we can move forward."

With tapping, you don't have to wait for life to push your buttons. You can sit down, bring up any issue that's bothering you, even if it's not bothering you at the moment. You can go fishing for things that you know bother you, and release it. Consciously, intentionally, and permanently.

Karma isn't mentioned in the Bible. Well, you won't find the word *"Karma"* in the Bible, but the idea is there.

Karma comes from Sanskrit, the sacred language of Hindu philosophy.

But the Truth it points to? That's universal. Karma isn't fate.

Karma isn't etched in stone. It's not your destiny or your fate. It's just energy, energy that's been heading in the wrong direction

The beautiful thing is, you can redirect it. You can release it. You can resolve it. Any time. Any place. No permission is needed.

Listen to your Soul. When you feel emotions like resentment, grief, or regret, that's your soul saying,

"This is ready to be released."

It's a signal, not a punishment.

Karma is not some angry force watching you from the sky. It's not trying to punish you. It's more like a mirror, showing you the effects of your own choices, so you can see clearly and return to love.

It says,

"This story isn't finished yet. Something needs closure."

And once you give it that closure, through love, through awareness, through tapping, your free.

Chapter 17

Go Into the Pain

Your subconscious mind believes it's in charge of how you feel. It uses your past experiences to decide when you should feel pain and how bad that pain should be.

The ego is built around this idea. It stays alive by controlling your negative emotions.

If you bring the pain into the light, you'll loose it for the rest of your life. When pain gets stuffed down, it doesn't go away. It festers and returns as physical illness.

The Ego's Trick

Your ego doesn't want you to face your pain, it wants you to avoid it. The ego wants to shake your bottle of muddy water and pretend there's less dirt since it's not setting on the bottom. But guess what?

The sediment is still there, it's just looking for another way to get your attention.

You have a better way now to clean this sediment. Now that you've learned how to tap, you have a new choice. You don't have to wait for pain to sneak up on you. You can go straight into it fully, and honestly.

Now you can dive into the pain with courage. Here's the amazing thing:

If you face this emotional pain completely, it can only last 9 seconds.

That's it. Feel the pain. It will pass.

If you would like, you can visualize your pain. Give it a shape that you think it has. If you have a pain, you can't face directly, you can create the equivalent to a straw man between you and the pain and tap out the straw man. You can even give it a name.

59

Daniel W. Wink

A Real Story

I once worked with a man who had just lost his son in a terrible accident. He couldn't even talk about it. The pain was too much to face. I ask him to give the experience a name. He said,

"The worst day of my life."

So we tapped out,

"Even though I just had the worst day of my life, I deeply and completely love and accept myself."

After a couple rounds of tapping he was able to talk about the accident in detail. We tapped it out. And he began the healing process.

What about judgment Day?

Some religions teach that after you die, there will be a Judgment Day, where God punishes you unless you've found atonement. Real atonement isn't about punishment. It means bringing light to something you once avoided. When you see your issue clearly, it's no longer a problem. It's just something you've outgrown

God Is Only Love

If God it pure Love, then He can't see anything bad in you. If He did, it would make him impure and that's not possible. The only thing that ever separated you from God was a misunderstanding.

The real *"Judgment"* isn't from God, it comes from you. It's self-judgment, self-blame, and shame.

When you release those emotions, something amazing happens: You realize you were never separated from God. *Forgive Yourself* if someone hurts you, remember: They were doing the best they could with the level of awareness they had at the time. And guess what? You have been doing the best you can too. That means your innocent too. Be gentle with yourself. Want to be forgiven? Forgive yourself.

God can only say, *"Yes"*. God does not argue with you. If you say,
"I'm a hopeless sinner," God says, *"Yes, you're right."*

If you say, "
I'm a divine child of God," God says, *"Yes you're right."*

Jesus said,
"All that I can do, you can do, and greater things."

What's the difference between Jesus and the rest of us? It's not that he was better, it's that he fully accepted his divine identity. You can too.

And you do it by letting go of emotional baggage. By clearing out the sediment from your drop of water. Tap it all out.

When I first started tapping I tapped on everything, even old movies. Let's be honest, TV and the movies program us emotionally.

Since the 1950's the C.I.A. and Hollywood have been working together to control the narrative. Operation Mockingbird is still going on.

That's more of the *"Deep States"* programming us.

I remember once, I was watching the movie, *"Jesus Christ Superstar."* My wife walked in the room and I was setting on the bed tapping away while I was singing,

,*"Tell me Christ, how you feel tonight. Do you plan to put up a fight?"*

The look on her face was priceless. Yep, I tapped everything. There is sediment hiding everywhere.

Hollywood and the Main Stream Media are designed to fill you with emotional charges. Is it effective entertainment?

Or is it manipulation and control by design?

Chapter 18

The Dark Night of the Soul

Almost everyone hits a point in their life where everything just falls apart. Nothing works anymore. The beliefs you once held, gone. Hope? Gone.

You wake up with anxiety, and depression becomes part of your daily life. You stop trusting yourself. You stop trusting the world. This is often how a spiritual awakening begins.

The life you were living no longer fits and deep down, you know something has to change.

When your young, life is simple. One memory stacked neatly on top of another. For example, Let's say grandma's house was blue. If someone told you their car was blue, your mind saw their car the same color as grandma's house. But as life goes on, it gets more complicated. You realize there are many shades of blue. Now the car becomes the color of grandma's house with a dab of ball park bench. The rabbit mind makes these kind of connections until it just can't keep up with them anymore.

Your mind builds a wall made of beliefs, assumptions, and rules, most of them hidden in your subconscious mind. Eventually, that wall becomes too complicated, and it collapses. That's called **"The Dark Night of the Soul."** That's the moment you realize,

All My Beliefs are failing me

Now imagine this collapse happening to everyone at the same time. Right before someone has a great spiritual awakening, they go through this kind of collapse.

The world is about to go through
"A Great Awakening,"
but for us to get there, we are going to go through a collective
"Dark Night of the Soul."
Most people won't be ready. They won't have the tools to handle the confusion and chaos that everyone will have to go through.

That's why I am writing this book. To give you the tools you'll need to cope with the changes as they unfold.

People are about to find out that everything they were taught was a lie. Everyone's minds are going to need to be restructured at the same time.

We must go through a collective "Dark Night of the Soul" to Reach "The Great Awakening"

#######

My Own Collapse

When I went through my own *"Dark Night of the Soul,"* it was brutal. I became so agoraphobic that to leave the bed I thought I was going to die. I lost my job, and my house.

I had a pregnant wife, three kids and every part of my body was screaming, *"I can't do this anymore."*

My oldest son just reached the age I was when I lose my dad. I guess the mind thought it was my turn to go.

That was my knees-hitting-the-floor-moment.

My body gave up. My mind gave up. My soul gave up. The only thing left that I could do was, surrender.

It was not an external surrender, like giving up my house, or giving up my job. It was an internal surrender.

After the surrender came the rebirth.

That was when My new life began. Some call it the second coming of Christ, not as a person, but as the rising and rebirth within the self.

Now when someone says blue. I see blue. I don't revisit grandma's house.

If I had known then what I know now things would have been a lot different.

It wouldn't have take 2 years out of my life.

That's a mistake we make all the time. We look back on the past and wonder why something happened then, based on the knowledge we have now. Instead of feeling guilty for mistakes made in the past, we should be grateful for the growth we went through since then, so we wont go through it again.

To be honest, if someone would have handed me this book before I went through my *"Dark Night of the Soul"* I probably wouldn't have read it. I was strong, I thought I could handle anything.

If that sounds like you right now, That's okay. If your not ready to dive in and do all the tapping yet, that's fine. Take this book and put it in a safe place. Put it with your survival supplies or your first aid kit. The day is coming when you will need it. When that day comes, you'll have it waiting for you.

A Course in Miracles say,

"Free will does not mean that you can establish the curriculum, It means only that you can elect what you want to take at a given time.

Chapter 19

Time to Clear the Sediment

I'm about to give you some pointers on where to find the sediment that needs to be cleared from your drop of water. Let's be honest; The world needs your clarity right now.

We have reached a point where there's no turning back. If I can save you even a little time on your journey, my mission will be accomplished.

In *"Power vs. Force,"* Dr. Hawkins tells us the average person only rises 5 points on the *"Map of Consciousness,"* in their lifetime if they are not actively choosing to grow. Why so slow?

Because of deeply ingrained patterns, karmic residue and unconscious resistance. And,

"The Deep State?" They want us stuck. They are doing everything in their power to keep us stuck. They don't want you to grow.

But here's the *"Good New,"* with tools like EFT, your growth doesn't have to be so slow. When you commit to seeking the truth, really commit, your devotion becomes the only judge of your limits. How high do you want to go?

Tapping gives us a radical means for growth. A way to speed up your awakening process like never before. and the *"Map of Consciousness,"* helps us clarify the direction we're heading.

Your not alone on your journey, even when you go within. A lot of people think their situation is unique. That their pain is unlike anyone else's. But the Truth is:

We all carry the same wounds. Childhood traumas, guilt, shame.

It's just the price we have to pay for being raised in a dysfunctional world.

You don't have to stay stuck. The issues I'll share in the next sections are the top reasons people go to therapy.

Many of these issues can be buried so deep you may not even know they affect you.

You don't need to analyze these issues at all. You just need to tap the different situations out and see what come up.

Instead of talking about your pains for years on a couch, let's tap them out. Talk therapy is slow if it works at all.

The ego loves therapy. It gets to talk about itself so it's not looking for a solution.

Tapping cuts through all that, tapping is faster and it works. If you are willing to go deep to find the root cause of your pain, you will be greatly rewarded. The issues will be resolved once and for all.

No repeat visited are required. Just freedom. So, let's do some house cleaning. Let's roll up our sleeves.

It's time to face what's been hiding in the back corners of our minds. We're not here to judge, we're here to clean. Ready? Let's get started.

Chapter 20

Mother Issues

Your mother didn't love you enough, get over it. Your not alone.

Everybody carries pain from their childhood. Some memories are right there on the surface. Others are buried deep, like they've always been a part of you. But if you want to grow and feel lighter, this is the stuff you have to clear out.

Start Tapping

Begin by tapping the karate chop point on the side of your hand and say:

"Even though my mother didn't love me enough, I deeply and completely love and accept myself."

"Even though my mother didn't love me enough, I deeply and completely love and accept myself."

"Even though my mother didn't love me enough, I deeply and completely love and accept myself."

Now go through all the tapping points from the top of your head, down through you face, chest, side, and wrist.
Let it out.

Do another round of tapping but this time, let's take it home.

"Even though my mother"

And let her have it. Finish that sentence with everything you've been holding on to.

Let it out. Cry if you want to. Get mad. Say the things you were too scared or afraid of saying in the past. The things that still hurt. The memories that sneak up. This is the time to unload. Don't be surprised if while you're tapping, memories pop up that you had forgotten all about.

There is no need to filter anything that comes up. You don't need to justify or explain anything to anyone about how your feeling, or about what is coming up.

Your not here to protect her or yourself, you're here to heal.

Remember to end your rant with,

"I deeply and Completely love and accept myself."

Go Deeper.

Was there someone else in your life that played a mother role to you? A grandma? An Aunt?

Are you a mother yourself?

Bring up any issues you may have about your own parenting skills.

Do memories or thoughts pop up that don't seem to make any sense? Like they are from another person? Tap those out too. They might be from a past life, or even a movie you watched.

Until around 8 years old, your subconsciousness mind records everything like it's happening to you. Did you see someone get beat? You have a recording of being beaten. That person could have been on TV. The child mind doesn't distinguish between truth and fantasy.

70

The Big Picture

This is why it's so important to protect your thoughts and emotions, especially those of children. Because the world isn't always gentle.

And yes, some groups want to keep us stuck in fear and pain. The *"Deep State"* relies on keeping us locked in our negative emotions. The more emotional pain we carry, the easier we are to control.

If your eyes swell up with tears while you are tapping, let them.

If your body starts to shake, let it. You're not breaking, you're clearing. You're releasing all the stuff your body's been holding onto for way too long. No matter what you say or remember during tapping your karate chop, end the set-up with:

"I deeply and completely love and accept myself."

This tell your inner self,

"It's okay. You're Safe Now. You Can Let Go.

As you proceed through all the tapping points from your head to your wrist, repeat statement that you said during the set-up. Use the ones that had the most emotional charge.

Go through this process as long as your getting an emotional charge. It will only be a few times before you find yourself becoming bored with something that was just a major deal to face.

Chapter 21

Father Issues

Your father didn't love you enough, get over it.
And I'm going to say it again, because it's important, your not alone.

We all carry old pains about our dads. Some of it is obvious. Some of it is buried deep. Either way, it's time to clear it.

Start with Tapping

Just like you did with your mother, begin by tapping on the karate chop point on the side of your hand and say,

"Even though my dad didn't love me enough, I deeply and completely love and accept myself."

"Even though my dad didn't love me enough, I deeply and completely love and accept myself."

"Even though my dad didn't love me enough, I deeply and completely love and accept myself."

Now go through the full tapping cycle: head, eyebrow, side of the eye, under the eye, under the nose, the chin, collarbone, under the arm, and the wrist.

When you go back for your second round like you did with your mom, look for and feeling of abandonment. When you were little he left you to go to work. Your child mind didn't understand where he was going. It just knew that he left you. Your subconscious mind remembers those feelings, even though they happened years ago.

It doesn't matter if it was last week or thirty years ago, it runs those old emotional records like it's happening today.

Now however, you have the tools to change these old stories and clean up the records.

As you tap, think back. Where there moments when you felt invisible? Times where he yelled at you, or just wasn't there? Did he seem more interested in work or sports? Did he seem interested in everything but you?

Bring those memories up. Let them rise. Say whatever you have to say, then tap it all out.

Let yourself feel the sadness or the anger. Let your body release it. And when it's time to cry, cry. When it's time to breathe deep, breathe deep. That deep breath after a tapping session is a sign something big just got cleared. You'll feel calmer, and more at peace.

You'll know that old pain is gone. Your more free to experience your own true light.

#######

If you are a parent, its' important that you apologize to you children. Apologize for any and all short comings you had in your parenting skills.

Children look to their parents as if they're Gods. If a parent gets mad, the child thinks they did something that mad them mad. Even if they didn't.

All they know is that they have become unworthy.

Children think their parents are infallible. Let them know you *DID* fail, and that your sorry. You didn't fail them intentionally. You did the best you could with the knowledge you had at the time. Let them know you're just human too.

Let them hear this come out of your mouth and don't just assume they know it.

They may say, ya, dad, we know, but they need to hear it. From You.

Chapter 22

The Fear of Death

It was the fear of death that got me stated on my spiritual journey so many years ago.

When I was a little boy I had to share a bedroom with my big brother. It seemed like every night he would find a reason to beat me up. While I was getting my beating he would say, **"I'm going to kill you."**

After he moved out of the bedroom I stopped getting my nightly beatings. What happened is my mind took over and since I wasn't getting my beating, it though it must be time for me to die. I would get this terrible empty feeling. I would just start screaming. I would run to mom crying,
"I don't want to die, I don't want to die."

This sent me on a spiritual journey that has taken me far from the Southern Baptist upbringing where it all started.

I just knew I had to find peace within myself, no matter where it took me. With that being said, Thanks Bill. If it wasn't for you, I would have never taken journey I'm so grateful I'm on. I'm sure many of you have similar stories

#######

If you've been doing the tapping exercises this far, you probably realize by now, you're not your body.

Every time you feel afraid, your body acts like something is being taken away from you. It's like going through a tiny version of death, over and over again.

Once you get over the fear of the big death, all those little deaths loose there meaning.

The Story I was Told Growing Up

You didn't exist until your mortal parents had sex. After that, you got this body to live in. Just one shot at life.

Your home, family, race, sex, and beliefs were all handed down to you, before you ever left your mother's womb.

Then your told to live you life *"Right"*, or when you die, you will go to hell for eternity.

Sounds pretty scary right? No wonder so many people are afraid of dying.

But Wait... Is that True?

If life is eternal, where were we before we were born?

Does Eternity really begin in the back seat of a car? I don't think so.

The truth is you did not *"Start"* to exist when you entered this body, and you will not *"Stop"* existing when you leave this body.

Death isn't the end. It's just a shift in what you're aware of. A new way of seeing. A new place to be.

So, The real question isn't, ***Will I still exist?"*** It's, ***"What will I experience next?***

#######

I did not lay out a tapping sequence here figuring you know enough now to figure out what needs to be said and how to do it.

If it's in question, say it and tap it. You can not do the process wrong. There is nothing you can not tap and there is no such thing as having a negative response from tapping.

As your talking to yourself pay attention to the sensations your experiencing around your eyes and forehead.

Say things that make your forehead feel puffy then tap it out.

Chapter 23

Life Doesn't Stop and Start

One of the biggest mistakes we are led to believe is that life is a series of beginnings and endings.

You wake up to a new day.

You go to work to begin another shift.

You watch the clock, waiting for the day to end. Even your evening TV time is broken into chunks.

Half-hour shows. Commercial breaks. On, off. Stop, start. This trains your mind to think in pieces. But life doesn't really work like that.

Life flows. Always moving, always now.

No matter where you go, there you are. You are more than a body trapped in time.

You are a spiritual being having a short physical experience. You came here to learn, to grow. And to learn, you needed a feedback system. So, you created a body. This body is like a mirror. It shows you what you're holding onto. All your thoughts and beliefs.

What Happens After Birth?

When you were born, your body was clean and balanced. I know not everyone was born with a perfect body; however, the body you received was the perfect body you needed to learn the lessons you came here to learn.

But then the programming started.

You started to believe you're just a body. Separate from others. Separate from Source.

And now, when life doesn't match your beliefs, you feel pain, be it emotional, physical, or spiritual. That's how the body gets your attention.

With this body you can experience when your thoughts are in disharmony with source. If you hold on to beliefs that say you're separate from God, you create stress and illness, because it's not true.

Your body will show you where these beliefs in separation live.

You can let go of these beliefs that are holding you back. You can choose connection instead of separation. You can choose truth over fear.

If you choose to hold onto your limited beliefs, that's okay. The chance to change will come back again, and again, until you do.

Because Love is patient. And life is eternal.

Chapter 24

The Belief in Specialness

The next thing to clear is all beliefs in specialness. This goes straight to the core of what it means to be in the world, but not of it.

We are trained to value being *"Special."*

Specialness is a lie

It's designed to keep us separate, alone. It's just another trick by the ego. What if we let it go?

If I could change one thing in this world, I would get rid of all

"Special Interest Groups."

Every single one of them. Even religions.

Being special always means someone else is less special. It creates walls. It says

, *"Us versus Them.*

" And that's not truth.

We are one body. We are not separate.

We're not fragments, we are one.

You and me? We're like cells in the same body.

Maybe you're a hand, and I'm a foot. We have different jobs. Different looks. But we're part of the same living system.

Same soul, Same ocean.

It makes no sense to say,

"I'm the most important wave." No, Dear. You are the ocean. So is everyone else.

Let's tap it out.

Tap away every thought that says you're more or less than anyone else. Tap out the need to stand out. Tap out the fear of being ordinary. Because underneath all this noise is peace.

Underneath all those costumes is your wholeness. And when you realize you're whole, you won't need to be special anymore. You'll just need to be.

Chapter 25

Nobody Cares

I spent 5 years, 9 day, and 2 and a half hours in the U. S. Army. In my 71 years, not once has a single person ask me what it was like to be in the Army.

Does that surprise you?

Now think about your stories. The ones you carry around like relics from the past. Some stories you have told a thousand times.

Others have never made it past your lips. In some, your the hero who overcame the impossible.

In others, you were the victim.

"This is why I am the way I am."
"If only they hadn't done that."
"If only life had gone another way."

But here's the truth: None of these stories matter. Not really. The only thing that matters is whether there's still an emotional charge connected to them.

Because if there is, and you're still clinging onto them, that charge is draining your energy. It's the toll you're paying to keep those stories alive.

And is it worth it? Let's be honest: most people really don't want to hear your stories anyways.

The next time you're in a group, pay attention. When someone is talking, how many people are truly listening to the person talking? And how many people are just waiting for that person to stop talking, so they can talk?

Most people are toned into their own private radio station:

W.I.I.F.M.   **What's In It For Me.**

So What do you need to Tap Out?

The belief that your stories matter to other people.
Because in most cases, they don't.

Now that doesn't mean stories have no value at all. Some do. Some are inspirational. Some will reach the right person at the right time and opens doors.

But even then, if there's emotional baggage attached to it, you still have to release it. Your healing doesn't depend on whether your story is heard.

Don't feel like your story has to be shared so others will understand you. They have their hands full trying to understand themselves.

Chapter 26

Rewiring Triggers

Let's say someone calls you a *"Bitch"* and it sets you off.

When you hear *"Bitch"*, instantly your vital force energy drains from your forehead and rushes down to your hands and feet in preparation for fight or flight.

Your subconscious mind thinks you're under attack. It thinks preparing you for fight or flight is the best job it has. It doesn't realize there could be another way to respond.

Whenever the subconscious mind has an option, it will always choose the path that is most beneficial for you. So, let's give it another option instead of fight or flight.

So let's say you know it bothers you when someone calls you a *"Bitch."*

Put your fingertips on your forehead and start saying, or thinking:

"Bitch, bitch, bitch. I'm such a bitch. Look at me being a big bitch."

Keep going, get ridiculous with it. Say whatever makes your forehead feel puffy.

Feel the pressure building? That's you sending the energy from your forehead down to your hands and feet in preparation for fight or flight.

With your fingers on your forehead, the energy will flow down through your arms, to your fingers, and back into your forehead. Your fingers are acting as a conduit.

The energy is returned to where it came from. Your subconscious mind will now have a **new record.** In the future when someone calls you a **"Bitch,"** your mind has a record of **not draining** the vital force energy, which is more beneficial, so it will choose this option in the future. No more upset feelings.

It is estimated that only about 5% of your thoughts ever make it to your conscious, level. A whopping 95% of your thoughts stay in the subconscious level.And the only ones that come up are your best thoughts. Could you imagine what's going on inside there?

In other words, you are consciously aware of only 1 out of every 20 thoughts you have.

The rest are like stealthy background programs quietly influencing your choices, emotions, and habits. Your body is still experiencing the effects of unconscious thoughts.

I've Made This Part of me Nightly Routine

When I lie down, I lay on my side and place the fingertips of my free hand on my forehead.

I just let my mind wonder where ever it wants to go. This clears up a lot of emotional baggage that never got to the conscious level.

If any concerns came up during the day, I'll revisit that now. This ends the day with one final house cleaning.

In my forehead I can feel a lot of movement going on. It's like a bunch of little guys moving furniture around.

Sometimes there's a sudden *jerk*, a *shiver,* or a feeling like something just *Popped*. That's not random. That's a **release**. That's **Grace at work**.

The body knows how to heal, and the soul knows what to keep and what to release.

Then I drift off to sleep, ready for dreams of peace, and whatever miracles tomorrow my bring

Chapter 27

The Power of Mantras

Using a Mantra is a beautiful way to create a home base for your wondering mind.

No matter where you go, there you are.

And what is it that goes everywhere with you? Your thought, your state of consciousness.

A mantra is like striking a bell, one that echoes through your nervous system, gently realigning your mind with truth.

It's your mental tuning fork.

A Mantra is your Home Frequency.

A Mantra work best when they're given time to carve a groove in your consciousness, like water etching stone.

Pick one that lifts your spirit.

One that reminds you of where you are going.

One that dissolves the fog and anchors you in the now.

Make your mantra your home base.

Train your mind so that when it wants to talk, it sings your mantra.

Let it become the background music of your thoughts.

Then, when life gets loud or off-center, just whisper your mantra, or even think it, and feel yourself return to your center.

Return to self.

Because your mantra isn't just a sound, it's a doorway.

A frequency,

A way home.

Chapter 28

Ad Rosem Per Crucem

Ad Rosem Per Crucem, Ad Crucem Per Rosem

Translates as:

"To the rose by the way of the cross. To the cross by the way of the rose."

This means to ascend from the cross, we must connect with the rose in the heart.

We find ourselves in a time like no other.

A time where sacred frequencies are no longer just poetic, they are essential tools for our transformation.

One such tool is this ancient vibrational frequency;

"AD Rosem Per Crucem"

"Ad Crucem Per Rosem"

This is a formula of spiritual alchemy.

The Rose symbolizes our divine potential.

Our sacred heart, our higher love.

The Cross symbolizes the trials, the ego, the density of earthly life.

Together, they reveal the holy path of transformation.

This is not a bypass.

It's not about avoiding pain or pretending the shadows aren't there.

It's about rising through sorrows, not around them.

The Rose blooms within the Cross. The soul unfurls in the body.
The lead becomes gold.

I first learned this sacred phase through

The Rosicrucian Order AMORC.

The Rosicrucian Order AMORC, is a *"School"* that teaches natural and cosmic laws.

I have heard people label this organization as a cult.
Like it's one of those evil secret societies that are trying to control the world.
Nothing could be further from the truth.
It is a *"School"* What some people want to label as secret is, that it is private in the way it does it's teaching. They want to keep their lessons clear in the way they are taught.

The reason the outside world wants to see it as being a secret society, is because it is divided into degrees. The degrees are to divide the lessons into levels. In normal schools, students in the tenth grade don't discuss what they're learning with students in the third grade.
Normal people would see that as normal.
Bad mouthing AMORC is just another way the *Deep State* likes to hide the truth behind false narratives.

Even the term or title *Illuminati* in it's original use was a good thing. It referred to the enlightened one. Those that had gone through the journey to find truth.
In 1776 Adam Weishaupt established a sect that he called the *Illuminati* that has no connection to the true meaning of the name.
This is just another example of how the evil in the world has been perverting the truth.

Chapter 29

The Last Stand of the Deep State

There is a war going on right now.

Not someday. Not metaphorically.

Now.

We are stepping into the final chapter of Earth as we know it. Leaving behind the familiar echoes of a world built on fear and separation. What lies ahead will not resemble the past, for the veils are thinning, the timelines collapsing, and the call to awaken can no longer be ignored. The old story is ending, not with destruction, but with revelation. What remains will be holy.

Gone are the days when we could afford the luxury of blind trust in our earthly leaders, believing they held our best interests at heart. In our slumber, we left the gates of our sovereignty unguarded, and in crept forces so cunning, so cloaked in illusion, they flourished in plain sight. Fed by our ignorance, and shielded by our denial. What we thought was order was, in truth, control. But now, the veil lifts. The soul remembers. And the time of holy discernment has come.

Not long ago, the very idea that our world could be under the grip of satanic, soul hungry forces seemed too dark, too unthinkable to entertain. It was easier to scoff than to see. But now the curtain has been pulled back, and here we are, standing in the harsh light of truth, eyes wide open.

What was once dismissed as conspiracy is being revealed as choreography, meticulously designed to keep humanity asleep, afraid, and obedient. But no more. What is seen cannot be unseen.

The evil we are confronting is not symbolic, it is real, and it has ruled unchecked for far too long. For millennia, the **deep state**, this shadowy priesthood of control, wove it's spell over humanity, chaining minds and harvesting souls in plain sight. But their reign of terror is ending. They have overplayed their hand. In their arrogance, they pierced the veil too far, awakening the very force they sought to suppress, the Divine within us. Now, the sleeping giants are rising, and this time, we remember who we are.

For generations, they chipped away at our sovereignty, wearing down the divine inheritance we hold as children of God. Quietly, persistently, they eroded our freedom, cloaking tyranny in the shadows, not out of humility, but to conceal the rot of their corruption. But in their hunger for power, they pushed too far. And in doing so, they exposed themselves. The mask slipped. The serpent revealed it's fangs. And now, the light they feared is shining straight through them.

To honor Lucifer, they were bound by a twisted code, one that required them to reveal their intentions, however subtly, so they did. They hid their rituals in plain sight, dressed them in satire, spectacle, and song. They passed off their darkness as entertainment, embedding confessions in comedy, weaving wickedness into lyrics, and portraying possession as pop culture. It was never about fiction, it was about permission. And with our laughter, our silence, and our unawareness, they believed we gave it.

Through sports and entertainment, the deep state believed they had us fully entranced, distracted just enough to keep our eyes closed and our spirits sedated. They fed us drama, idols, and tribal rivalries, while behind the curtain, they played their true game, control. As long as we stayed invested in the spectacle, we were too hypnotized to notice the theft of our freedom, the poisoning of our minds, and the selling of our souls. But the trance is breaking. The spell is lifting. And the watchers are becoming warriors.

We've walked this path before. Civilization after civilization has risen to this precipice, reaching the heights of power, technology, and control, only to collapse under the weight of its own spiritual blindness. The earth bears witness in stone and ruin, silent reminders that when man's industrial might outpaces his inner knowing, destruction is inevitable. Great cities turned to dust. Towers built in pride now lie broken beneath the vines. We are not the first to forget the soul in pursuit of the machine, but we may be the first with the chance to remember before it's too late.

Our civilization teetered on the edge, poised to become just another layer of dust, another mystery for future generations to unearth and wonder, *"What went wrong?"* We came perilously close to becoming the next collection of ruins, concrete graves of forgotten wisdom and warnings carved in stone. But something shifted. A spark. A cry. A remembering. And now, against all odds, we are rising, not just to rebuild, but to redeem.

But this time, the tide has turned. And for the first time in the long and weary history of this planet, God wins. Not in secret. Not in symbols, but in full, radiant view. The darkness that once reigned from the shadows is being cast out by the rising light of awakened hearts. The war is not only won, it is being remembered as already over. The kingdom is not coming, it has arrived. And it lives within us.

We are waking up. The fog is lifting, and the light is breaking through the illusion. What once hid in plain sight is now seen for what it is. The **Deep State,** so confident in its control, overstepped its bounds. In its arrogance, it exposed itself, forgetting one eternal law: When darkness becomes too bold, it calls forth the light. And Now, humanity is no longer sleeping. We've remembering. And we're rising. With the rise of the internet, a divine loophole opened, a crack in their control grid. Suddenly, truth began to flow across borders and boundaries, reaching hearts and minds they never expected to awaken.

These satanic architects of deception could no longer bury the evidence or rewrite the narrative fast enough. This time, their distractions weren't enough. Their poisons couldn't sedate us. Their spells couldn't hold. We saw. We Shared. We remembered. And once remembrance begins, their game is over.

This time, let us awaken, truly and together. Let us rise as one body of light and bring an end to the evil that has ruled this world since the dawn of time. No more bowing to fear. No more hiding in silence. We came here for this very moment, to dissolve the shadows with the power of remembrance, to reclaim the earth for the children of God. The time of separation is over. The time of sovereignty has come. And with hearts united in Truth, we declare: the reign of darkness ends now.

God is with us. And this time, God wins. Not someday. Not maybe. Now.

Chapter 30

The Sigil

You may have noticed a special symbol throughout this book. It's round, golden, and mysterious, like something from an ancient scroll. That symbol is called a **sigil** (pronounced SIH-jil), and it's here for a reason.

A sigil isn't just a fancy drawing.
It's a symbol filled with **intention**, like a message that goes straight to your heart, without needing words. It's a bit like a logo, but instead of representing a company, it represents **energy, purpose,** and **remembrance.**

This book wasn't made just to share ideas, it was made to spark something deep inside you. Not just in your thoughts, but in your **consciousness.** So, I asked in prayer and meditation:

"How can I include something that will help people remember who they are, even if they don't read every word?

The Answer was clear.

"Create a symbol. Let it hold the vibration of awakening. Let it carry the energy of Truth."

That's when the sigil began to form.
Little by little, the image came together:
Each part means something.
But even more important is **how it feels.**

A circle for wholeness and unity

A cross for transformation and higher truth

A rose for the heart and the unfolding of inner wisdom

Light, movement, and sacred balance.
Looking at the sigil slowly should help you feel calmer. That's not imagination, that's your inner self responding to energy in language deeper than words. Symbols speak directly to the subconscious mind.. They go around the busy thoughts and head straight for the soul.

This sigil holds the energy of

Spiritual Truth

Inner Power

Awakening

Peace

Every time you see it, it gently reminds you:
You are light. You are connected. You are already enough.
This sigil was made with care. **With Love.**
Not to impress the eye, but to *impress the soul. It's a Silent prayer* printed on the page.
A *visual mantra* you can return to again and again.
Whenever you see it, remember:
You are part of something ancient and beautiful. You carry truth within you.
You are never alone. And no matter what's happening in the world...

The light has already won.

Epilogue

We were born into a world at war-though most never knew it. The battle was never truly about flesh and blood, borders or politics. It was for consciousness, for the soul of humanity. For eons, darkness ruled through deception, whispering lies through systems we were told to trust. We were programmed, poisoned, and pacified.

And yet... we endured.

Within each heart, a spark remained, a fragment of the Divine, unextinguished. Generation by generation, that spark was passed like a sacred ember. And now, in our time, it ignites.

We are waking up.
We are remembering who we are, and whose we are.
We are seeing through the illusion, calling out the lies, and standing where once we knelt.

We are reclaiming our sovereignty, not from governments Or tyrants, but from the fear that kept us small.

This time, the story ends differently.

Because God is not coming back.
God is rising from within.

In every heart that chooses truth over comfort, love Over fear, and courage over silence.

This is *"The Great Awakening."*

And this time..."*God Wins.*"